SURVIVOR STORIES™

EARTHQUAKE

True Stories of Survival

Greg Roza

rosen publishing's
rosen central®

New York

For Sulu

Published in 2007 by The Rosen Publishing Group, Inc.
29 East 21st Street, New York, NY 10010

First Edition

Library of Congress Cataloging-in-Publication Data

Roza, Greg.
Earthquake : true stories of survival / Greg Roza. – 1st ed.
p. cm. – (Survivor stories)
Includes bibliographical references and index.
ISBN-13: 978-1-4042-0997-8
ISBN-10: 1-4042-0997-2 (library binding)
1. Earthquakes – History. 2. Survival skills. I. Title.
HV599.R69 2007
363.34'95–dc22

2006018934

Printed in China

On the Cover: On October 18, 2005, a man from Balakot, Pakistan, sits on the rubble that–before the earthquake–was his brother's shop. He fears that his dead brother is buried beneath him.

CONTENTS

This survivor sits in front of his collapsed house in Muzaffarabad, Pakistan, on October 13, 2005, five days after the earthquake. Like many people affected by the quake, he had nowhere to go after his home was destroyed.

INTRODUCTION: WHAT IS A DISASTER?

A disaster is an event that causes destruction, hardships, injuries, and deaths. Many types of disasters happen every year all over the world. Natural disasters are often unpredictable and swift. For this reason, they can cause tremendous devastation. Man-made disasters can be just as destructive. Regardless of the causes, all tragedies are harmful events that can cause sadness for hundreds, thousands, and even millions of people.

Earthquakes are among the most devastating natural disasters. Earthquakes occur when the enormous plates that make up the earth's surface slip over or crash into each other. The interaction between plates causes tremors that radiate out from the point of contact. These tremors are earthquakes, or a violent shaking of the ground. Earthquakes can be nearly unnoticeable, lasting for less than a second. Or they can be powerful and deadly, lasting for more than five minutes.

The strongest earthquakes can tear down buildings, open deep cracks in the earth's surface, and cause destructive landslides. Earthquakes that occur at the bottom of the ocean can cause giant waves called tsunamis. When tsunamis hit land, they leave extensive destruction and death in their wake. In addition to these dangers, earthquakes often result in difficult-to-contain fires.

People who are lucky enough to survive may suffer nonetheless. They commonly lose a friend or relative; many survivors experience multiple losses. This alone can make coping with the aftereffects of an earthquake tragic and agonizing. Many survivors also lose their homes and are forced to find new places to live. Strong quakes can isolate an area by knocking out its lines of communication and transportation. Aftershocks, fires, and poor weather can make surviving the aftermath of an earthquake even more difficult.

During the Kashmir earthquake of October 2005, thousands of people lost their homes and farmland, and most knew at least one person who died. Landslides severed many of the lines of communication, and most roads were impassable. It was therefore difficult, and nearly impossible at times, to reach the areas that were hit the worst. Aftershocks continued for a month, increasing the damage.

Although the Kashmir quake was larger than most, these are the kinds of conditions that survivors must commonly overcome. Despite the sorrow and danger inherently linked with earthquakes, remarkable stories of survival also frequently emerge. Survivors often defeat great odds by escaping the ravaging effects of a disaster. Their stories tell us much about the human ability to overcome tragedy and misfortune.

1
THE KASHMIR EARTHQUAKE OF 2005

On October 8, 2005, at 8:50 am, an earthquake measuring 7.6 on the Richter scale struck between Pakistan and India, in the mountainous region of Kashmir. The epicenter of the quake was about 65 miles (105 kilometers) north-northeast of Islamabad, the capital of Pakistan.

The people of Kashmir, who have been at the center of a dispute between Pakistan and India for more than sixty years, have a long history of hardship. The region is located atop a fault line between two major tectonic plates and is therefore plagued with frequent earthquakes.

Most of the communities in the region are small, and the buildings are simple brick and wood structures. The majority of these buildings—including homes, schools, and hospitals—collapsed during the quake. Aftershocks caused further damage and panic. More than 87,000 people died, and an estimated 3.5 million were left homeless. Some sources estimate the cost of damages to the area to be well over five billion dollars.

LANDSLIDES IN THE NEELAM VALLEY

Ahsan Haque was traveling in a car with friends through the Neelam Valley when the earthquake occurred. The driver suddenly announced that the car felt like it was flying and he could not control it. Then they noticed a landslide falling down the slope next to their car. At a fork in the road, the driver was able to steer away from the tumbling rocks and drive under a bridge.

A landslide blocked the road between Islamabad and Muzaffarabad, Pakistan. Ahsan Haque *(inset)* and his friends were traveling in the Neelam Valley when the quake occurred, and luckily escaped unharmed.

Rocks crashed down on either side of the bridge as Haque and his friends looked on in horror. The landslide raised a cloud of dust so thick, it looked like the land around them was boiling. When it was all over, the friends celebrated, having thought they narrowly survived the largest landslide that had ever occurred.

However, shock set in as they continued on their way toward the city of Muzaffarabad. Many of the roads they approached were closed due to landslides. Soon they noticed survivors crawling over huge boulders that blocked the road. Many were carrying injured children. Only now did the young men understand that there had been an earthquake. Haque and his friends had packed many supplies for their trip through the mountains, and they began to help the survivors any way they could. Before local police were able to arrive, they had set up a makeshift relief camp. When Haque and his friends finally arrived home in Lahore, Pakistan, a few days later, their families were overjoyed to find that they were alive and well.

DISASTER IN ISLAMABAD

The earthquake struck quickly, leaving people very little time to escape buildings. Even in Islamabad, Pakistan—about 62 miles (100 km) southwest of the epicenter—several structures tumbled to the ground. A ten-story apartment building fell, trapping survivors inside. One survivor reported being woken up by the quake. He and his bed had

This image, taken on October 8, 2005, in Islamabad, Pakistan, shows one of the two Margalla Towers reduced to rubble. The ten-story building collapsed in seconds during the earthquake, trapping as many as 120 people.

been thrown against the ceiling as the building came down. He lived on the top floor, which may have been lucky since he was not crushed in the collapse.

When the dust began to settle, people rushed to the building to help those trapped inside. The scene was a horrific one. Some witnesses reported hearing the weak cries of survivors calling out for help. Rescuers began digging through the rubble with their hands. Soon cranes were brought in to lift the heavy slabs of concrete, many of which were smeared with blood. One survivor was removed from the rubble only after his legs were cut off. In the days that followed, crowds of Pakistanis cheered each time one of the eighty-nine survivors was pulled from the rubble.

SCHOOLS COLLAPSE

Relief agencies estimate that thousands of children died during the quake. Many of them were buried under the rubble of their schools. UNICEF (The United Nations Children's Fund) estimates that hundreds of schools collapsed and approximately 17,000 schoolchildren died as a result.

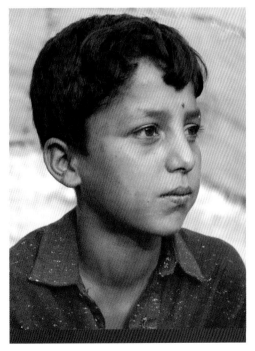

One of the lucky survivors in the Pakistani village of Bugarmong was eleven-year-old Mazhar Hussein. When the earthquake struck, his teacher told the students to run out of the classroom. Mazhar dove under his desk, as did the students on either side of him. As debris poured down,

Mazhar Hussein *(above)* was eleven when the earthquake struck. He survived his school's collapse, but many classmates died.

Mazhar thought he was going to die. When the quake ended, the boy was trapped under the rubble that had been his school. He called out for help, and his teacher came to unbury him. The classmates who had surrounded him were dead, and Mazhar had to scramble over them as he escaped the debris.

Farina, another survivor, was thirteen years old when the quake struck, flattening the city of Balakot. Farina's school also collapsed

while she and her classmates were inside. Farina's first thoughts were of her family. She dug through the rubble to save her two younger sisters, Misbah and Laraib. Next she rushed to her sister Sayra's classroom. Her mother joined her there, digging through the bricks and cement, desperately searching for Sayra. They eventually found her, but unfortunately it was too late. Sayra had died.

After surviving her school's collapse, Farina (*top center*) dug through the rubble to find her sisters. She found two of them, but was unable to save another, her sister Sayra.

THE LAST SURVIVOR

Rescuers continued to search for survivors for many days after the quake struck. After about a week, however, they began to lose hope of finding more survivors. Now came the difficult task of finding and burying the dead.

As for many people, this was the case for Muzzafar Hussein, a forty-year-old farmer from the village of Pahl, located high in the mountains of Pakistan-controlled Kashmir. He had been visiting a farm miles away when the earthquake occurred. He rushed home to find that a landslide had covered his home, farm, and family. Every home in the village had been destroyed, and 250 of the town's 600 inhabitants had died.

With the help of his three surviving sons, Muzzafar spent twelve agonizing days clearing rubble. During this time, he uncovered the bodies of his wife, son, and three daughters. He came to realize that he might never find the body of his missing son, Khalid.

On November 5, twenty-seven days after the earthquake,

On October 13, 2005, five days after the earthquake, rescue workers were still searching for survivors in Balakot, Pakistan.

Muzzafar's son Zahid found Khalid's hand reaching out of the debris. Muzzafar was astonished to find that, although he was in very bad shape, Khalid was alive. He had been pinned beneath the debris with just enough room to move his hands. His leg was badly broken.

Five days later, a vehicle finally arrived to take Khalid to the nearby city of Muzzafarabad where he would receive medical attention. Doctors were amazed that Khalid had survived for so long without food or water. They treated him for his broken leg, but this was not the worst of Khalid's injuries.

Khalid no longer spoke. Even though his eyes were open, he appeared not to see those around him. His father sat by his bed, stroking his head, while Khalid's hands dug at the air and clawed at his blankets—as if desperately trying to escape from beneath a pile of rubble. Khalid was in a tragic state of shock. Doctors are not sure if Khalid will ever recover from the psychosis he developed while pinned beneath the rubble.

2
THE SAN FRANCISCO
EARTHQUAKE OF 1906

On April 18, 1906, San Francisco, California, was devastated by an earthquake. This disaster was one of the worst ever to hit the United States. The magnitude of the earthquake was about 7.6 on the Richter scale. The quake, which began at 5:12 AM, lasted about forty-five to sixty seconds. It was felt as far north as Oregon, as far south as Los Angeles, and as far east as Nevada. The earthquake was the result of a rupture of 296 miles (476 km) of the San Andreas fault line, which stretches along the coast of California. In San Francisco, fires that began because of the earthquake raged uncontrollably for three days, adding substantially to the destruction.

Many people jumped out of their beds that morning, awoken by the tremendous shaking as well as the sounds of screaming, breaking dishes, and cracking foundations. Thousands of dazed San Franciscans struggled to understand what was happening. Many buildings had tumbled into the streets, and most of the others were damaged beyond repair. Fires raged in many sections of the city. Aftershocks continued to frighten the city's residents for the next twenty-four hours.

Survivors of the 1906 quake stand at the top of Sacramento Street, watching the fires rage in downtown San Francisco. Notice that the front of the building on the far right has crumbled into the street, revealing the building's interior to passersby.

Nearly every home in the city was uninhabitable. Women and children huddled in doorways and in rows of tents, many of which were provided by the military. Some women even gave birth in these tents and doorways. Healthy men were required by police and military authorities to help in any way they could, and many hauled debris away until they collapsed from hunger and exhaustion. Due to severed gas lines, all cooking had to be done in the streets. Buildings were demolished to help reduce the severity of the fires and further injuries.

After the earthquake, survivors had to cook in the streets. In the foreground, children watch as a woman cooks on a makeshift stove made of bricks. In the background is a relief camp that was set up by the U.S. Army.

Police and army officers prohibited people from returning to their homes and businesses because the buildings were too dangerous. As a result, many people lost everything they had owned, including valuables, family heirlooms, photographs, and even pets. People left the city any way they could, carrying what they could and

Hundreds of survivors were forced to flee the burning city on foot.

helping the injured as much as possible.

Initial reports estimated that about 700 people had died in the quake and its aftermath. Today, most experts believe that more than 3,000 people lost their lives. Approximately 28,000 buildings were destroyed. About 250,000 people were left homeless.

BUILDINGS TUMBLE

Thomas Jefferson Chase was a ticket clerk who was walking to work when the earthquake struck. Chase remembered hearing a low rumble as he walked. Then the tremors hit with a fury. Stunned, Chase stood and watched as buildings on both sides of the street buckled and crumbled. He saw a brick building fall and knew there would be no survivors. Great clouds of dust rose and blocked his view of the destruction. Power lines and trolley cables snapped like threads and fell a few feet away from him. They hissed and jumped dangerously. Bricks and glass came raining down around him, yet he remained motionless and in shock.

As the first tremor ceased and the dust settled, Chase moved to the opposite side of the street. Then another tremor hit, throwing him to the cobblestones. More bricks and glass came down around him. After the second tremor eased, he hurried down the street before a third one hit.

Chase reached a cross street and was amazed to see the extent of the destruction. The front wall of one apartment building had fallen completely away, revealing the rooms within as if it were a giant dollhouse. The street was full of people who had just escaped the surrounding buildings. Many were barefoot and in their pajamas. They looked around in disbelief, some crying, others moaning in pain from injuries. Shortly after this, Chase saw smoke rising from the fires that would quickly consume the city.

HELPING OTHERS THROUGH THE DISASTER

Emma M. Burke was the wife of an attorney and a resident of San Francisco. Her detailed description of the earthquake appeared in *Overlook Magazine* on June 2, 1906. Burke related an in-depth account of the aftermath to readers. She was lucky that her home merely sustained damages. The Burkes were forced to cook their food in the street that day, and Emma did her best to feed the people passing by. She let a mother and daughter who had lost everything– and could barely stand from hunger and exhaustion–use her home.

The Burkes slept in a nearby park. Fires burned in the center of the city two miles away, and the night sky was bright with their light.

The next morning, Emma's husband, Bart, was put in charge of water conservation and distribution. This was a difficult job since so many water mains had burst and there was limited water to go around. The Burkes returned to their home during the day for supplies, and they continued to care for and feed those who needed help. They watched nervously as the fires moved closer. On the fourth night, a man on horseback rode by, announcing that the fires were finally under control. The following day, the Burkes returned to their damaged home.

For the next few days, the Burkes did what they could to help others despite the fact that they, too, had lost so much; Bart's law building had burned to the ground. They fed people, clothed them, and helped the injured. Soon they were able to tour the devastated city center. Stores, churches, museums—everything lay in ruin. Despite the destruction, however, Emma was amazed by the human compassion she witnessed and the ability of her neighbors to pull together during a time of need.

A BOY IN THE RUBBLE

DeWitt C. Baldwin was just eight years old when the 1906 earthquake occurred, but he remembered the entire ordeal very clearly when he related it to a friend at the age of eighty-eight. He recalled that he had risen at about 5:15 AM to prepare for his piano lesson when the first tremor hit. He sat on his bed as dishes crashed and furniture moved about the room. DeWitt dressed hurriedly and ran downstairs. His family ate a quick breakfast while they discussed what they would do. Suddenly another tremor struck. Shortly afterward, they heard the local fire alarms. They had received a few reports about what had happened from neighbors. DeWitt's father rushed off to his job while his mother, older sister, and baby sister stayed in their house; it was one of the few that had not suffered serious damage in the quake. DeWitt anxiously rushed out to see what was burning.

DeWitt C. Baldwin was about five years old in this photograph, taken three years before the earthquake he remembers so well.

He discovered several fires in his neighborhood, including a nearby department store. Before he reached the fire, however, DeWitt came upon the first of many demolished buildings. The first floor of a local hotel had sunk halfway into the ground below it; the second and third stories had tumbled into the street.

Baldwin recalled that he did not feel scared, just curious. He raced around the debris and shell-shocked people, learning as much as he

On April 20, 1992, DeWitt C. Baldwin *(center)* and family members stand by the fire hydrant that was used to save Baldwin's community from the fires. The hydrant—which is one block from Baldwin's childhood home— receives a fresh coat of gold paint every year on April 18.

could about the earthquake. He saw firefighters struggling to contain raging fires. He saw buildings in rubble and open cracks in the streets, some 25 feet (7.6 m) deep. He saw flocks of people carrying posses- sions they had rescued from their destroyed homes. Over the next few days, he watched as the buildings of San Francisco burned or were torn down. He watched long processions of people leave the city on foot, carrying their belongings and injured family members. Martial law (temporary military control) had been declared, and soldiers patrolled the streets to stop looters and to help keep order. One even threatened to shoot Mrs. Baldwin when she lit a candle inside their dark home.

On the fourth day, fires were still raging. The Baldwins were forced to evacuate their home and head for the safety of the surrounding hills. They were lucky enough to have a wagon to carry their belong- ings. As he and his family left the city, the seriousness of the situation finally started to weigh upon the boy. He was sad to leave the city and sad to see his fellow San Franciscans in so much pain and sorrow. As the Baldwins rode their wagon out of town, Dewitt felt bitterly sorry for those around him who did not even have a wagon. He wondered where these people would find food, shelter, and water. The Baldwins were one of the lucky families. But DeWitt C. Baldwin would always remember the 1906 San Francisco earthquake as the day his world was changed forever.

3

THE GREAT KANTO EARTHQUAKE OF 1923

On September 1, 1923, at 11:58 AM, a powerful earthquake struck the Kanto Plain on the Japanese island of Honshu. The quake lasted for six minutes. Some reported it had a magnitude of 7.6 on the Richter scale, while others reported that it was closer to 8.3. Whatever the exact magnitude, the disaster caused widespread destruction throughout the Kanto Plain region and devastated the cities of Tokyo and Yokohama. In some areas, the ground reportedly raised about 24 feet (7 m) into the air. Over the next few days, between 200 and 300 aftershocks occurred.

More than 150,000 people lost their lives during the Kanto earthquake; about 40,000 were never found. Over 570,000 homes were ruined, and in Tokyo alone, approximately 1.5 million people were left homeless. The loss of lives was tragically high for a number of reasons. Many structures in the Kanto region—including a good portion of those in Tokyo—were old wooden buildings built upon loose soil instead of solid bedrock. As a result, many people died as their homes crumbled around them, and many more lost their homes.

Taken in the days after the earthquake, this photograph shows the destruction to Tokyo's Akasaka residential district. The buildings, made primarily of wood, toppled easily. Many burned in the fires following the quake.

The epicenter of the earthquake was beneath Sagami Bay, south of Tokyo. This resulted in a quickly moving tsunami that hit beaches and bridges within minutes of the quake. Waves taller than 43 feet (13 m) washed over the beach of Atami, an area south of Tokyo. When the waves receded, sixty people had been carried to their deaths, along with 155 homes, most of which had been destroyed by the quake. Mudslides and landslides caused by the earthquake buried homes and whole communities in nearby mountainous regions.

Numerous fires started as a result of the initial quake. Since the earthquake struck just before lunchtime, a large number of families and workers were at home preparing food. In Yokohama, nearly ninety fires broke out. The quake severed water lines, which made it difficult or impossible to fight the fires. In addition, high winds from a nearby typhoon caused the flames to spread quickly, causing as many as 100 firestorms to sweep through the affected cities. In some areas, the fires continued for two days. Reports of the disaster state that fires claimed as many as 91,000 lives—more than the quake itself.

FIRSTHAND ACCOUNT

According to his account excerpted by the Earthquake Engineering Research Center, Otis Manchester Poole, a manager at a British trading firm in Yokohama, was at work in his office when the earthquake hit. He became aware of the earthquake as his office began to sway, and he heard the "vicious grinding of timbers." Soon Poole felt the entire building move beneath him. The floor did not just shake according to Poole, but rather it "heaved, tossed and leapt." The walls bulged "like cardboard" around him, sending paintings flying to the floor. Finally the building began to disintegrate, and hunks of the plaster ceiling crashed all around him. The quake lasted about four minutes, but to Poole, it seemed like forever. Remarkably, Poole emerged from his ruined office without injury.

Top: The Dodwell & Co. Tokyo staff (Otis Manchester Poole is fourth from the right). **Bottom:** The ruins of the Dodwell & Co. office after the earthquake. The men in the foreground are trying to uncover a vault that was buried in the debris.

LIVING THROUGH A FIRESTORM

In one of the most tragic and horrifying developments of the disaster, about 40,000 people died during a firestorm in the middle of Tokyo because they had nowhere to run. Bensaku Morita was seven years old when the earthquake occurred. He had been working as an apprentice in a jewelry shop. When the quake struck, Morita and the shop owner's family ran to a vacant lot in the center of Tokyo. Others were doing the same thing. Many people had brought their belongings with them, including clothes and furniture. The lot became very

This postcard shows the Hanjo area of Tokyo *(inset)*. The larger image shows what the firestorm looked like at the Hanjo clothing depot and its surrounding area.

crowded; estimates say that as many as 40,000 people squeezed into the vacant lot.

By about 4 PM, the sky had become dark and stormy. A fire was approaching from the south. When a strong wind blew in, the lot suddenly became engulfed in swirling flames. The winds had created a firestorm that took over the crowded lot. The air became unbearably hot, and it was difficult to breathe. Morita recalled that people were being blown through the air like leaves while debris rained down. Fearing for his life, Morita soaked his shirt in a puddle and used it to cover his mouth. He laid face down while the firestorm raged around him for close to two hours. When the fires calmed down, Morita's back was bleeding, and burned bodies surrounded him. He had no idea how he survived the ordeal when so many lost their lives.

VIOLENCE AND RACISM

Another dangerous situation that resulted from the Great Kanto Earthquake was a wave of violence spurred by fear and racism. Rumors about the causes of the fires spread quickly. Some stated that there were Koreans taking advantage of the chaos by looting, starting fires, and committing other crimes. Some were reported to have bombs. In addition, much of Tokyo's well water had become cloudy, which is a common occurrence after an earthquake. Not knowing this, some Japanese accused Koreans of poisoning the water. The Japanese government enacted martial law across the country, and some people have accused the government of allowing these rumors to spread. The false reports resulted in more deaths. Many Japanese tried to protect Koreans, but most Japanese believed the false reports. Initial estimates stated that more than 200 Koreans and a handful of Japanese had been murdered, but many experts claim the number is between 6,000 and 7,000.

Fear of an Angry Mob

Mun Mu Son, a Korean teenager, lived with her family in Tokyo when the earthquake occurred. After the quake, they were very scared of being murdered due to the false reports. They took shelter in an uncle's home. At one point, a group of Japanese men armed with hooks and swords barged into the house. Luckily, her uncle's landlord convinced the angry mob that Mun Mu Son's family had been with him all day and were innocent.

However, this was just the beginning of the terror. A friend of her father's decided to publicly protest the acts of violence. Later that day, Mun Mu Son was horrified to see a rowdy group of Japanese parading the streets with her father's friend's head on the end of a pole. Although they had survived the quake, the fires, and the collapsing buildings, Koreans like Mun Mu Son were more afraid of the Japanese mobs. For many days, they remained in fear for their lives.

No Place for a Child

Surviving the Kanto quake was a harrowing experience. Children, however, may have had the hardest time. A fourteen-year-old boy named Masao had been at a movie theater with a friend when the first tremors hit. What he then witnessed gave him nightmares for years. Masao recalled that people were falling out of the theater's third-floor balcony. He and his friend managed to escape the theater, although both suffered injuries. In the streets, they stepped over rubble and dead bodies as they fled. Terrified, they took shelter in a building. Masao heard a strange sound next to him and turned. To his horror, he discovered that a heavy sheet of iron had fallen onto his friend and killed him.

Masao's terrifying experience continued as he then witnessed gangs of Japanese attacking Koreans. He took refuge at an uncle's house and frequently heard the gangs outside. Even though he was Japanese himself, groups of angry people several times demanded that he prove it. One group made him read a passage of Japanese text to make sure he did not have a Korean accent. On another occasion, a gang of men accused him of being Korean and hiding behind a mask. (His face was bandaged due to his injuries.) Luckily for Masao, his uncle saved him from the mob. Unfortunately, thousands of Koreans were not as lucky. To this day, Koreans who survived the ordeal are still waiting for an official apology from the government of Japan.

4

THE TANGSHAN EARTHQUAKE OF 1976

On July 28, 1976, at 3:42 AM, an earthquake struck the Hebei region of China. Ninety-three miles (150 km) of a fault line that ran beneath the city of Tangshan ruptured, causing an earthquake with a magnitude of 7.8 on the Richter scale. In just ten seconds, most of Tangshan, which at the time had a population of about one million people, lay in ruins. The epicenter of the quake was 6.8 miles (11 km) below Tangshan. Tremors were felt as far as Xi'an, China, approximately 470 miles (756 km) away.

Fifteen hours after the earthquake, an aftershock that measured 7.1 on the Richter scale struck, increasing the damage and loss of life. Some survivors of the initial quake were still trapped under rubble, and most of them died as a result of the major aftershock.

Despite having a fault line running through the city, Tangshan was not designed to withstand an earthquake. Most of the buildings were made of brick and were not reinforced to endure seismic forces. After the quake, approximately 85 percent of the buildings were in ruins or uninhabitable. Collapsed railways, bridges, and roads kept rescuers

Roads, bridges, and railroads buckled during the quake, making it difficult for rescuers to enter the city—or survivors to leave. This image, taken the day of the quake, shows survivors trying to cross a collapsed bridge.

from reaching survivors quickly. Electrical, water, and sewage systems failed, making the situation even more difficult for survivors.

Unlike most earthquakes, there were no foreshocks (small tremors that occur before an actual earthquake strikes) prior to this one. The quake occurred in the middle of the night, while most people were in bed, unaware and unprepared to react. Homes and buildings collapsed on top of people while they slept. Many died without even waking up. Since power was knocked out, initial rescue efforts were hindered.

Coal miners working in a nearby mine, for example, were trapped underground for over two weeks.

At the time, the official death toll estimate for the quake was more than 240,000 people. Today, however, some experts believe the number is closer to half a million. Approximately 7,000 families disappeared as a result of the quake. In addition, about 700,000 people were injured. These numbers make the Tangshan quake the most deadly earthquake in modern times.

QUICK AND DEADLY

All earthquakes with a magnitude higher than 7.0 are capable of great destruction. The Tangshan quake lasted only about ten seconds yet flattened an entire city, burying hundreds of thousands of people in the rubble. Relatively few people were outside during the quake, and few were able to describe the destruction as it occurred.

A middle-school teacher reported that he woke to a sound that he thought was rain. He went outside to cover some of his belongings. That is when the earth began to rumble. The teacher tried to run back to warn his family. He heard a loud boom and was thrown to the ground. He watched as his house twisted from side to side and the roof was raised up. He was thrown back about 15 feet (4.5 m). When he looked up again, his house and the others around it had collapsed and were replaced by a thick cloud of swirling dust.

Li Rong remembered the quake vividly. Like many people, she was in bed, asleep. When Li was awoken by the violent tremors, things were falling all around her. She tried to move but could not. She was pinned beneath the remains of her home. She remained trapped for several hours before her husband and children—who had been at work—arrived to dig her out.

SURVIVORS AND RESCUERS

The quake was so sudden and powerful that it left hundreds of thousands of people trapped beneath wreckage. It took two days for army units from nearby provinces to arrive and help dig out survivors. They did not have the machinery necessary to move large debris. Instead, they used their hands to dig out survivors. The first rescuers to begin digging were the estimated 200,000 to 300,000 survivors who had been able to crawl out of debris themselves. These people rescued an estimated 80 percent of the survivors left trapped in the rubble.

One of those survivor/rescuers was a man named Wu Tien-pin. His father had pulled him out of his home. His face and back were injured during the quake. Instead of seeking medical attention, however, Wu left his ruined home to help rescue trapped neighbors.

Wu quickly organized survivors into teams of rescuers. As Wu and a small number of others dug through the rubble with their bare hands, additional rescuers joined them. In about five hours, they

The earthquake of 1976 literally flattened the city of Tangshan. About 90 percent of the residential buildings collapsed, trapping many people beneath the wreckage. Above, survivors work to clean up the rubble.

saved hundreds of victims. Despite Wu's acts of bravery and leadership during the disaster, however, he was unfortunately unable to save his own wife and three children.

IN THE COAL MINES

At the time of the quake, the industrial city of Tangshan had eight coal mines. The earthquake damaged about 58 percent of the mines. Many of the mines were cut off from the earth's surface, and some became flooded. Ventilation and electrical systems were destroyed, and rescuers were afraid that the survivors would die from a lack of oxygen. In many cases, rescued miners themselves took on the responsibility of rescuing their fellow workers. Remarkably, only thirteen of the 10,000 coal miners working during the earthquake died.

Deep in the Pit

In one instance, more than 600 miners were trapped at the bottom of a pit 1,700 feet (518 m) deep. When the quake struck, the miners were shaken deep beneath the earth's surface, and the electricity was knocked out. The air became hot and stale, and water was slowly seeping into the pit. Rescuers needed to come up with a plan to save these men before the rising waters drowned them.

Lacking any other plan, they lowered a metal ladder down into the pit using a hand-powered winch. Once the ladder reached the bottom, fourteen miners climbed on and they were slowly hauled out. Then the ladder was lowered once again to pick up another fourteen miners. The rescue operation was slow, and the work was back-breaking. Each load coming up out of the pit weighed more than a ton (.9 metric tons), and the men powering the winch tired quickly. Rescued miners took turns powering the winch until, ten hours later, all 600 miners were safely aboveground.

One of the Lucky Ones

Meng Jiahua, a fifty-two-year-old coal miner, was working underground at the time of the earthquake. Meng and his coworkers suddenly felt the earth shake all around them. When they exited the mine, a frightful sight greeted them. Most of the buildings, for as far as they could see, had collapsed, and rubble was everywhere. Meng saw lines of survivors—many of them injured—on one side of a road and lines of dead bodies along the other.

Not all of the surviving coal miners were as lucky. Some spent as many as fifteen days underground with no food or clean water. When the workers were finally rescued, they were exhausted and famished.

FOREIGN REPORTS

The Communist government of China was, and still is, very secretive. Rather than reach out for help, it preferred to keep Chinese affairs hidden from other countries and to proclaim that the country was self-sufficient. The Chinese government lied to the rest of the world about the death toll and size of the devastation caused by the quake. Due to this secrecy, people today still dispute the actual death toll.

Reports of the destruction leaked out mainly from foreigners who had been visiting Tangshan at the time of the quake. A group of French ambassadors had been staying in a hotel just outside of

Tangshan. Like others in the city, they awoke to see strange lights in the sky just before the quake struck. To this day, no one is sure what caused these lights.

The French ambassadors quickly fled the hotel as the tremors started. The hotel crumbled to the ground just as they escaped. Remarkably, only one of the Frenchmen died in the quake. The survivors reported that they had wandered barefoot around the leveled city in a daze. The previous day, the city had been bustling with Chinese citizens. Now a mere handful of people stumbled through the rubble. One French survivor recalled that the only structure standing after the quake was a single smokestack in the distance. Similar reports of widespread devastation became common as the world came to hear about the quake. It is still considered to be one of the most destructive natural disasters in modern times.

This photograph, taken on the day of the earthquake, shows the overwhelming destruction it caused.

GLOSSARY

aftershock A small earthquake that follows a larger one after a period of calm.

bedrock Solid rock beneath a layer of soil.

Communist A follower of Communism, which is a political system that advocates the communal sharing of wealth and property.

demolish To destroy a building or structure completely.

epicenter The exact location on the earth's surface directly above the focus of an earthquake.

evacuate To remove people from a dangerous place.

fault line A crack in the earth's crust caused by the movement of tectonic plates.

firestorm A large, intense fire sustained by inward rushing winds that feed a rising column of hot air.

foreshock A slight tremor or small earthquake that precedes an earthquake.

habitable Fit to be lived in.

looter Someone who engages in stealing in a time of war or disaster.

magnitude A measure of the energy of an earthquake.

martial law Temporary military rule of the civilian population in times of emergency.

psychosis A mental disorder that is characterized by lost contact with reality, hallucinations, and incoherence.

racism The belief that one race is superior or inferior to others.

Richter scale A scale from 1 to 10 used to indicate the strength of an earthquake. An earthquake is said to have a Richter magnitude.

seismic Having to do with earthquakes.

tectonic plate A large segment of the earth's crust that moves in relation to the other segments.

tremor A shaking or trembling movement felt during an earthquake.

tsunami A large destructive ocean wave caused by an underwater earthquake.

typhoon A violent tropical storm in the western Pacific and Indian oceans.

winch A machine used for hauling or pulling a heavy load.

FOR MORE INFORMATION

The American Red Cross
2025 E Street NW
Washington, DC 20006
(202) 303-4498
Web site: http://www.redcross.org

The Canadian Red Cross
170 Metcalfe Street, Suite 300
Ottawa, ON K2P 2P2
Canada
(613) 740-1900
Web site: http://www.redcross.ca

Federal Emergency Management Agency (FEMA)
500 C Street SW
Washington, DC 20472
(800) 621-FEMA (3362)
Web site: http://www.fema.gov

Multidisciplinary Center for Earthquake Engineering Research
University at Buffalo, State University of New York

Red Jacket Quadrangle
Buffalo, NY 14261
(716) 645-3391
Web site: http://www.mceer.buffalo.edu

Museum of the City of San Francisco
PMB 423
945 Taraval Street
San Francisco, CA 94116
Web site: http://www.sfmuseum.org

United States Geological Survey (USGS)
John W. Powell Federal Building
12201 Sunrise Valley Drive
Reston, VA 20192
(888) ASK-USGS (275-8747)
Web site: http://www.usgs.gov

WEB SITES

Due to the changing nature of Internet links, Rosen Publishing has developed an online list of Web sites related to the subject of this book. This site is updated regularly. Please use this link to access the list:

http://www.rosenlinks.com/ss/earth

FOR FURTHER READING

Johnson, Rebecca L. *Plate Tectonics* (Great Ideas of Science).
Minneapolis, MN: Twenty-First Century Books, 2006.

Reed, Jennifer. *Earthquakes: Disaster and Survival.* Berkeley Heights,
NJ: Enslow Publishers, 2005.

Sandler, Martin W. *America's Great Disasters.* New York, NY:
HarperCollins Children's Books, 2003.

Spencer, Christian, and Antonia Felix. *Shake, Rattle, and Roll: The
World's Most Amazing Volcanoes, Earthquakes, and Other
Forces.* Hoboken, NJ: John Wiley & Sons, Inc., 1997.

Tanaka, Shelley. *A Day That Changed America: Earthquake!* New
York, NY: Hyperion Books for Children, 2004.

Van Rose, Susanna. *Volcanoes and Earthquakes.* New York, NY:
Dorling Kindersley, 2004.

BIBLIOGRAPHY

After the Tangshan Earthquake. Peking, China: Foreign Languages Press, 1976.

"Aged Survivor Jolts Collective Memory of Tokyo's Fatal Day." TaipeiTimes.com. September 24, 1999. Retrieved April 12, 2006 (http://www.taipeitimes.com/News/insight/archives/1999/09/24/3843).

Baldwin, DeWitt C. "Memories of the San Francisco Earthquake and Fire." Virtual Museum of the City of San Francisco. Retrieved April 11, 2006 (http://www.sfmuseum.net/1906/ew8.html).

BBC News. "Escape from the Epicenter." October 11, 2005. Retrieved May 30, 2006 (http://news.bbc.co.uk/1/hi/world/south_asia/4330696.stm).

Becker, Jasper. "Remembered with a Shudder." *South China Morning Post.* July 7, 1996. Retrieved April, 2006 (http://special.scmp.com/chinaat50/Article/Fulltext_asp_ArticleID-19990928191042300.html).

Burke, Emma M. Virtual Museum of the City of San Francisco. Retrieved April 11, 2006 (http://www.sfmuseum.net/1906/ew13.html).

Chase, Thomas Jefferson. Virtual Museum of the City of San Francisco. Retrieved May 27, 2006 (http://www.sfmuseum.net/1906/ew1.html).

Denawa, Mai. "Behind the Accounts of the Great Kanto Earthquake of 1923." Brown University Library. Retrieved April 18, 2006 (http://dl.lib.brown.edu/kanto/denewa.html).

James, Charles D., and Carol Cameron. "The 1923 Tokyo Earthquake and Fire." Earthquake Engineering Research Center. Retrieved April 24, 2006 (http://nisee.berkeley.edu/kanto/tokyo1923.pdf).

Lloyd, Anthony. "Earthquake Survivor Lay Buried for 27 Days." Times Online. November 18, 2005. Retrieved May 30, 2006 (http://www.timesonline.co.uk/article/0,,25689-1877858,00.html).

Nance, John J. *On Shaky Ground: An Invitation to Disaster.* New York, NY: William Morrow and Company, Inc., 1988.

Reese, Lori. "An Ominous Rumbling." Timeasia.com. September 27, 1999. Retrieved April 21, 2006 (http://www.time.com/time/asia/magazine/99/0927/tangshan.html).

Schenk, John. "A Child-Friendly 'Activist from the Heart.'" World Vision. Retrieved April 20, 2006 (http://www.worldvision.org/donate.nsf/child/pakistan_stories_activist).

Schenk, John. "I Thought We Would Be No More." World Vision. Retrieved April 20, 2006 (http://www.worldvision.org/donate.nsf/child/pakistan_stories_no_more).

U.S. Geological Survey. "The Great 1906 San Francisco Earthquake." Retrieved April 17, 2006 (http://quake.wr.usgs.gov/info/1906).

Yong, Chen, et al., eds. *The Great Tangshan Earthquake of 1976.* Elmsford, NY: Pergamon Press, 1988.

Zeilinga de Boer, Jelle, and Donald Theodore Sanders. *Earthquakes in Human History.* Princeton, NJ: Princeton University Press, 2005.

INDEX

ABOUT THE AUTHOR

Greg Roza is a writer and editor who specializes in creating library books and educational materials. He lives in Hamburg, New York, with his wife, Abigail, his daughter, Autumn, and his son, Lincoln. Roza has a master's degree in English from SUNY Fredonia.

PHOTO CREDITS